What Does *That* Mean?

A Dictionary of Death, Dying and Grief Terms for Grieving Children and Those Who Love Them

By Harold Ivan Smith & Joy Johnson

Design by Janet Sieff
Youth Editor: Paris Jennifer Sieff

A Centering Corporation Resource

©2006
Centering Corporation
All Rights Reserved.

ISBN: 1-56123-196-7

To order the books quoted in this resource go to www.centering.org.

Phone: 1-866-218-0101

Centering Corporation
PO Box 4600
Omaha, NE 68104

D1418379

Table of Contents

With thanks to Elliott Culver Keller and Anna Culver Keller,

Earl Grollman, Donna Schuurman, Peggy Boehm, Richard Gilbert,

Darcie Sims, Helen Fitzgerald, Arvil Pennington, Nancy Keller,

Marilyn Mokhtarian, Dr. Sally Higgins, Valerie Bosco

and Dr. Jay Harrison.

Getting Started

For Parents and Others Who Love Grieving Children

I like good strong words that mean something.
Jo in **Little Women** by Louisa May Alcott

Victoria Alexander says it is important for people to find the words to express their losses. Yet words mean different things to different people. Remember this exchange between Humpty Dumpty in **Through the Looking Glass**? When Humpty Dumpty says, "When I use a word, it means just what I choose it to mean – neither more nor less." Alice protests, "The question is, how you can make words mean so many different things."

Grieving people of all ages need words to verbalize and talk about their losses. We all need words to comfort grievers. So what does a word mean?

Words can comfort and affirm children and words can confuse or frighten them. Alice is right. Words mean different things to different people. Most children have a smaller vocabulary with which to describe their feelings. Children hear certain words and confuse them with other meanings.

Consider, in a child's world, **Mourning** and **Morning**; **Dead Body** and **Dead Wrong**. And there's the common word, **Terminal**. You can talk about life-ending illness or an airport using the same word.

Words mean more than what is set down on paper.

It takes the human voice to infuse them with shades of deeper meaning.
Maya Angelou in **Quotations for Kids**

Right. It isn't just the words alone. Our emotions, our tone of voice, our body language accompany those words and give additional meanings. Think of the ways we can say, "I love you."
>   I **LOVE** you.
>   I love **YOU**!
>   I love you.
>   I love you?

Now imagine accompanying that well-known phase with hugs or hands on hips or head in hands – weeping, laughing; saying it in anger, gentleness, fun. Meanings scurry around us like little dogs chasing a toy.

Our words and actions need to be helpful and clear because if you are part of a grieving family, the child will protect you. We have found that nearly one hundred percent of the time, children will protect and try to help the grieving parent. Children often hold onto their own grief until they see the adults around them grieve in healthy ways. During this time of sorrow and even longer, the impact of words and the emotions that accompany them can last far beyond childhood.

Arthur, age six, witnessed his father's anguish as he was told his mother had died. He thought if he asked questions it would further upset his father – nor would he ask them in the months and years to come. As an adult, Arthur said, "I don't remember grieving over my mother. She died and life moved on."

"My father told people how my response to the news, as he sat crying his eyes out between my brother Johnnie and me, was simply enough. 'Don't cry, Daddy,'" I consoled him. "As long as we have each other, we'll be alright." I don't remember any of that.

If Arthur's father had known to tell his son it was okay to cry and ask questions; that they would be sad for a long time and that his job was to be a child and not take care of him. If he had said, "Yes, son, we have each other. We'll be all right. In the meantime, ask questions, cry when you need to cry, get hugs when you need hugs and talk about your mother all you want. Let me tell you what happened and how your mother died and what we will be doing in the next few days . . ." things might have been different. As it turned out, Arthur developed a reputation as aloof. Some said this aloofness was influenced by the death of his mother and a beloved grandfather, both within a year. "I have understood that this quality of emotional distance in me may very well have something to do with the early loss of my mother. I have never thought of myself as having been cheated by her death, but I am terribly, insistently, aware of an emptiness in my soul that only she could have filled."

Children need to know the meaning of words. They take things literally and need explanations. There is an old story about a boy who wanted to go to the funeral home after his grandfather died. His father said, "No." The boy insisted. Finally the father gave in. The youngster walked into the funeral home, looked into the casket and exclaimed loudly: "He's still got his head!" When asked what he meant, the boy replied, "You said Pap-Pap's body was at the funeral home. I thought something happened to his head!"

Be aware, too, that present dictionaries for children do not always define death, dying and grief words well. One child was told her mother had died with hepatitis. She checked the dictionary and found, "A disease associated with needles." "Oh," she concluded, "My mother died from sewing our clothes." That little girl grew up to be comedienne Rosie O'Donnell.

The aim of this book is not to answer every question posed by a grieving child, but to bring honest answers and insights. It is only a guide. When talking to your child, trust our own intuition and judgment. We quote from a lot of children's books. They are all available from Centering Corporation, whose website and phone number are listed on the first page of this book. Our words are arranged alphabetically with other associated words beside them. We haven't found every word, either. You'll have some space to write in the words we missed. And there is more you can do:

> Read about grief.
> Attend a support group if possible.
> Enroll your children in a center for grieving children if there is one near you.

Grief is a part of life, when a death occurs, children need to know they are an important part of the family during this most important time. We can best protect children by answering their questions and letting them know we're there for them.

As you look up words for your child in this book, or if your child herself is reading it, keep in mind certain things:

Ask, "What is the child really asking?"

Remember the old story of the little boy asking where he came from? Dad responded with details of eggs and sperm, then the little boy said, "Oh. I just wondered. Mickey said he came from Cleveland." Watch your child as you explain. You can usually tell if you're on target. If you feel you are not on target, ask your child some questions.

Expect developmental differences.

How a 5-year-old understands dead is different from a 10-year-old and a teen. You know your child and can tell when she is bored or not "getting it." And remember, they'll want more information as they grow up.

Ask, "To whom is this child listening?"

Parents, teachers, parents of friends, grandparents, neighbors, daycare teachers, Sunday school teachers, coaches and kids are all likely to have their own definitions and explanations. Many won't be in sync with yours. You may have to deal with, "Ryan says it was God's will that Robbie died." Is that what you want your child to believe? If not, sit down, take the child on your lap and simply start out with, "That may be what she believes. This is what I believe," and go from there. When you share your beliefs with your child, you are making that child a real part of your life.

Make it safe for your child to ask questions about dying, death and grief.

Too many children think asking questions will make you uncomfortable or sad. In the movie, *Sleepless in Seattle*, Dr. Marsha Fieldstone asks 8-year-old Jonah if he has talked to his father about his mom's death. Jonah says, "No. It would only make him sadder." Let the child know nothing they can say or do will make you sadder. Let him know you grieve together.

Discount what they see on television.

After his uncle was buried, Elliott asked, "Now do we go read the will?" His mother said, "No. They only do it that way on TV." And you already know how actors who die in one show turn up in another. Let the child know television distorts death.

Tell the child the truth.

If you lie, fudge, stall or wax creative, the child will know. They are people-readers. They will find other sources and that could make your job more difficult. Kids can handle a lot if they're treated with respect, support and honesty.

Re-Answer.

Some questions are never final. Many will ask the same question over and over. It takes awhile for answers to sink in sometimes. As a child grows older, the question may pop up in another form. Bright children may ask questions or want comprehensive explanations we would expect from an older child or adult.

Work on your own definitions.

It's okay to say, "I don't know the answer to that one, but I'll find out." Feel free to ask funeral directors, hospice workers, clergy, psychologists and physicians what words mean. A part of adulthood is to keep learning and your children are excellent teachers.

Be surprisable.

Sometimes children offer insights that initially surprise us. Be open to being confronted by the wisdom of a child.

We wish you well on this interesting journey you are taking with your family. May all of you grow as you grieve. Remember: Grief is the price we pay for loving. The truly bereaved are those who never love.

A Dictionary of Death, Dying and Grief Terms for Grieving Children and Those Who Love Them

Accident

Say it: AXE-a-dent

You may hear someone say, "That was a terrible accident" when something happens that wasn't meant to happen.

Accidents happen every day. Some accidents happen when something goes wrong and you don't do it on purpose.

Most accidents don't hurt anyone: "Oops – I spilled my soup."

Sometimes accidents hurt for a little while: "I wiped out on my roller blades and hurt my leg."

And sometimes, accidents can cause death. "My uncle was in an automobile accident and died. My dog ran out in front of a car and got killed."

When someone dies in a really bad accident – like a car wreck or plane crash or other serious happening - that means they were hurt so badly that nothing the doctors and nurses or emergency teams could do helped. The accident made the person's body stop working. This kind of death can be hard because it comes as such a surprise and no one had time to say good-bye or tell that person how much they were loved.

Sometimes living things become ill or get hurt.
Mostly, of course they get better again, but there are times when they are so badly hurt
or they are so ill that they die because they can no longer stay alive.
This can happen when they are young
or old
or anywhere in between.

Lifetimes by Bryan Mellonie and Robert Ingpen

9

AfterLife

Say it: Af-ter-life

The belief in some kind of life after we die.

You may hear someone say, "I know I'll see him again some day." Or, "Grandpa is in Heaven now."

Many religions believe a part of us, often called SOUL or SPIRIT lives on after the body dies. This is an old, old belief.

Ancient Egyptians and some Native Americans as well as other peoples buried supplies, food, jewelry and money with the body for use after death.

In many religions, people think HEAVEN is God's home where people go after they die. There are different beliefs about Heaven. Some of your family may picture Heaven one way, and others think of it as something very different. Many people think of Heaven as a place of great peace, where no one is ever sick or hungry, sad or lonely, afraid or left out of things. No one hurts anyone or gets hurt. Some think Heaven will be filled with laughter and music.

God's special friends in Heaven are called ANGELS.

Many people are sure their pets are in Heaven, too. After all, what would it be like without dogs, cats, hamsters, birds, turtles and fish?

Many people find comfort believing they will see their loved one again when they, too, die.

Carl Sagan, a great scientist said, "I would love to believe that when I die I will live again, that some thinking, feeling, remembering part of me will continue." You may hear people talking about REINCARNATION (Re-in-CAR-nay-shun). You may hear someone say, "People die and then they come back in a different body to learn more lessons." That's a belief in reincarnation.

Some people believe that dying is like walking through a door into a place we can't see when we are alive.
These beliefs are important.
It is important for you to know them.
Beliefs help us when someone dies. Dying may be like a new beginning.
It is good for you to know about endings and beginnings. It is good to know about living and dying.

Tell Me, Papa by Joy and Dr. Marvin Johnson

Ambulance

RESQUE SQUAD/HELICOPTER

**Say it: AM-bue-lance
RES-Q-squad
HEL-a-cop-ter**

Special cars and trucks to take care of people who are in accidents or who become very sick very fast. Ambulances often come to the place where an accident happened with sirens blaring loudly.

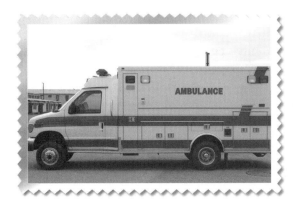

Often a fire truck is there, too, even if there isn't a fire. The fire truck comes in case a fire starts and sometimes it has special tools or equipment that can be helpful.

You may hear someone say, "The helicopter came to the accident and took him to the hospital."

Sometimes special helicopters fly to where an accident has happened and take the injured people to the hospital very quickly.

The inside of the ambulance and helicopter is like a tiny emergency room – that special place in a hospital where injured or hurt people are taken to help them just as fast as possible.

If you visit a hospital or a fire station, often they'll let you look inside the emergency room and inside the ambulance, too.

Sometimes, even though the helicopters and ambulances and fire trucks rush to where an accident happened, the people who were hurt don't live. They were injured so badly that nothing could make them all right again. They died. Sometimes they died right away. Other times they died in the hospital or even on the way to the hospital.

*Ms. Lee turned to the class.
"I just had a call from Tony's grandmother," she said.
Tony and his family were in an auto accident last night.
Tony's father and mother were hurt and taken in an ambulance to the hospital.
They'll be all right.
I'm sorry to say that Tony was killed."*

The Class in Room 44 by Lynn Bennett Blackburn

11

Anniversary

Say it: Ann-a-VERS-ar-ie

A special day where we remember or celebrate something important that happened.

You may hear someone say, "We always plant flowers on the anniversary of Mother's death. We will never forget her."

Your parents and grandparents may have celebrated a wedding anniversary. When you talk about something special you did a year ago on that day, that's an anniversary, too.

Just as we have birthdays, we have death dates or death anniversaries. Some people visit the grave of the person who died and leave flowers on the death anniversary.

Jewish families call the death anniversary YARSHZIET (your-site), others call it YEARMARK (year-mark) and light a candle the evening before that burns for 26 hours.

Some people may say you shouldn't remember or honor the anniversary. "Try not to think about it," they may say. But how can you not think about someone you love who has died? You remember them for the rest of your life.

There are a lot of things you can do to mark the anniversary of your loved one's death: If your person was buried close by, you can visit the grave. You can have your person's favorite meal or make a special cake. You can share memories with your family. You can do something different that you think of yourself.

Story: Andrew Jackson, the father of the seventh president of the United States, died in 1767, just months before his son Andrew was born. Young Andrew's mother, Elizabeth Jackson, died in 1781 when Andrew was only 13 years old. Andrew was then an orphan. Mrs. Jackson had been the most important person in her son's life. She admired him, believed in him and encouraged him. He would remember and treasure his mother for as long as he lived, especially while he was President.

Autopsy

Say it: AW-top-see

After a person dies, a doctor called a PATHOLOGIST (path-OL-o-gist) carefully opens up the body to see if she or he can find what caused the death. An autopsy is a lot like a surgery.

You may hear someone say, "We won't know the cause of death until after the autopsy."

In a surgery, the person is given an ANESTHESIA (an-es-THEE-cee-uh) – a special medicine that makes the person sleep while the surgery or operation is going on. Millions of boys and girls and grown-ups have surgery every year. The big difference is that during surgery we are alive. All our body parts are working. It's like we're in the deepest sleep possible. We do not wake up at all during surgery. After awhile we wake up and usually the surgery has fixed whatever was making us sick.

In the autopsy the body is opened up and every part is looked at so the doctor can tell if the person's heart made him die, if his lungs stopped working first, or if the person was killed. Doctors can tell just what it was that caused him to die.

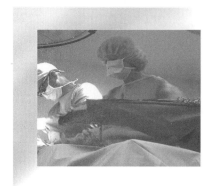

There may be several people around when an autopsy is done. Every state has someone called a CORONOR (COR-or-nor) or MEDICAL EXAMINER (med-ic-al X-AM-in er). This person is the pathologist's boss or supervisor.

Often an autopsy helps families and friends understand just why a person died. Often police use an autopsy to help catch criminals. Often an autopsy helps student doctors learn about the parts of the body. Sometimes an autopsy is called a POSTMORTEM (post-MORTim). "Post" means after. "Mortem" means death. So "Postmortem" is the operation done after death.

After the autopsy, the parts or organs are put back inside. The body is closed up so carefully that you would never know an autopsy took place.

Children have minds. They have imaginations. If they are told the truth in a loving and caring way, and if they are allowed to express their grief, they are capable of accepting even the most painful and devastating losses that life has to offer.

The Grieving Child by Helen Fitzgerald

13

Bereavement

Say it: Bee-REEVE-ment

Bereavement is what we go through after someone dies. It's all the experiences and all the feelings, too.

You may hear someone say, "Bereavement is a part of life. Everyone is bereaved at some time."

After someone dies a lot of things happen. We feel a lot of feelings. If we could take all the feelings and put them in a little box, we could call that box: **GRIEF**. There's a bigger box, too. That box holds the little box, GRIEF (greef) and a lot of other stuff besides. The big box could be called bereavement.

The big box of bereavement holds decisions that have to be made. It holds getting used to being without that person. It holds all the firsts that come after a death: The first holiday without your person. The first birthday. The first time you go somewhere you used to go to together.

The big box of bereavement holds a lot of newness and getting-used-to plus all the feelings that come with grief.

The word, bereavement is very, very old. Hundreds of years ago, bereavement came from the word, reft which meant to be robbed or have something stolen from you. In a way, that's how it feels when someone we love dies. We feel something has been taken from us. We've been robbed. We're BEREFT (bur-reft).

Grief and bereavement take a long time.
Sometimes it seems as if they'll never end.

Keys to Teaching Children how to Cope with Death and Grief by Joy Johnson

Bereavement Counselor
Bereavement Support Group

Say it: Bee-REEVE-ment Count-sell-or
Bee-REEVE-ment sup-ORT groop

Someone who has gone to school to learn how to help people after their loved one has died. A support group is made up of several people who are grieving.

You may hear someone say, "Talking to a bereavement counselor can really help. And the people in the support group became my best friends."

There are a lot of special counselors:

> School Counselors
> Ministers
> Psychologists
> Psychiatrists
> Social Workers
> and Bereavement Counselors.

A bereavement counselor will listen to people whose person has died. She will help them understand their feelings. She will help them decide what they want to do now that their person is gone. She will help them find new friends and new things to do.

Sometimes counselors meet with several bereaved people at the same time. This is called a BEREAVEMENT SUPPORT GROUP. There people talk about their feelings, their plans and their ideas. They learn about grief and bereavement. There are even support groups for children. When we go through bereavement, we are not alone. A lot of people are grieving at the same time. There are many special people who know how to help, or support us.

If at all possible, give a support group a try; even for just one session. And if at all possible, find out if there is a center for grieving children near you. Children need to know they aren't alone in their grief, and a center has trained facilitators who can act as wonderful bereavement counselors to your child.

Keys to Teaching Children how to Cope with Death and Grief by Joy Johnson

15

Body

Say it: Bod-ee

What is left of the person after that person dies.

You may hear someone say, "We're going to the funeral home to see the body."

We use the word, body, for both living people and dead people.

When you are alive, your body is active and working all the time. You run and jump. You breathe in and out. You eat and sleep and go to the bathroom.

After someone dies, all that is left is the body. Another word for the body is CORPSE (korps). This word is not used much anymore. You are more likely to hear it on television than in real life.

Always remember, a dead body cannot think or feel anything at all. A dead body never hurts or has pain. A dead body is just a shell.

If your family has an open casket, you can see the body.
The body will look as if it's asleep.
You can tell the difference between being dead and being asleep.
If your family has an open casket, you can touch the body if you want.
It will feel cool and the skin will feel firm.
It will feel a lot like the cover of this book, smooth and cool.
It's all right to look at the body or the casket as much as you want to.

Tell Me, Papa by Dr. Marvin and Joy Johnson

Burial

Say it: Bear-e-all

After a person has died, we need to care for the body. Often we bury the body in a place called a CEMETERY (SEM-a-tare-ee). **This means placing the body carefully in the soft, welcoming earth.** People have done this for thousands and thousands of years.

You may hear someone say, "Burial will be at Graceland Cemetery right after his funeral."

First the body is gently washed by special people and prepared for the grave. GRAVE is another important word for you to know. The hole where the body is placed in the ground is called a GRAVE (gur-ave). The hole is dug very deep and wide enough to hold the CASKET (kas-kit) and VAULT (valt). You can learn more about those words later. Burial is also called Internment (in-TURN-ment).

After the person's body is placed inside the casket, the casket is sealed shut very, very tightly. The casket goes inside the vault that is inside the grave. Maybe you've had little dolls where one doll fits inside another and then that doll fits inside another. Toddlers have little toy cups that fit inside one another. Your kitchen has measuring cups that fit snuggly inside each other, too.

That's how it works when a body is buried. The body is gently placed in the casket. The casket is placed inside the vault. The vault is inside the grave.

Then the grave is filled in with the soft dirt from which it was dug. Now the body is buried.

Not all bodies are buried in the earth. Even though they aren't under the ground, we still call it being buried. Some bodies may be buried in a building made just for bodies. That building is called a MAUSOLEUM (Maw-so-LEE-um).

Remember, when a body is buried, that person is dead.
That person cannot feel anything or think anymore or breathe in and out.
None of the parts in the body are working.
The person cannot see or hear because that person is no longer alive.
At the cemetery, the casket holding the body is lowered into the ground.
Waiting for it is a large cement box. This box is called a vault.
It protects the casket and keeps it dry.
The vault is shut and sealed and again, very, very slowly, the body returns to the waiting earth.

A Child's Book About Burial and Cremation by Earl Grollman and Joy Johnson

Caregiver

Say it: CARE-giv-ver

Someone who takes care of another person who is sick or dying. Often this is a family member.

You may hear someone say, "My mom and my aunt Lucy were my granddad's caregivers before he died."

Some people talk about caregivers being everyone who takes care of the sick person:
>Doctors
>Nurses
>Hospice workers
>and others who come to the home and help do things that are needed.

Every day Miss Angela drove up in her old blue car right at 11 o'clock to help Grandmother with her bath and pour medicine from a brown bottle for Grandmother to take.

Lilacs for Grandma by Margene Whitler Hucek

Casket or Coffin

Say it: Kas-kit

The special box in which the dead person's body is placed before it is buried.

You may hear someone say, "Grandma had a beautiful casket. I helped pick it out."

The casket is usually made of really fine wood or metal. There are many, many kinds of caskets and they come in all different sizes. Caskets can be covered inside, or lined with silk or other cloth. The cloth may be arranged or gathered in a beautiful way on the top of the inside. There is even a pillow for the head, even though the body inside cannot feel it.

On the outside of the casket there are handles so it can be carried. When you visit a funeral home, maybe your family will ask the funeral director to let you see some of the caskets. They are usually in a room of their own so family members can walk through and choose just the right one to hold the body of the person who died.

One kind of casket is called a COFFIN (koff-in). A coffin has six sides. It is shaped more like the body than a casket. It is smaller at the bottom, larger through the middle and smaller at the head. Coffins are used more in other countries than in the United States.

Families can also choose to have an open or closed casket at the funeral. With an open casket, people can see the body of the person who died. With a closed casket, the body cannot be seen because the casket lid is shut. Caskets are often kept closed when the person has died in a bad wreck or has been sick for so long the body is damaged.

One of the things Mama said made a funeral special was the casket. Mama said a casket is a beautiful box that holds the person's body. She said we could help her pick one out for Daddy. I thought it should be yellow and have sunflowers all over it to show how Daddy loved yellow. Mama smiled and said she wasn't sure they made yellow sunflower caskets, but maybe we could find another way to show Daddy's favorite things. We finally chose a casket that was simple. It had shiny gold handles that reminded me of the way sunflowers look in the sun.

Sunflowers and Rainbows for Tia by Alesia Alexander Greene

Cause of Death

Say it: Kaw-se of deth

Why someone died.

There are many causes of death. Some people die of NATURAL CAUSES (Nat-ur-al Kaw-ses). They could die naturally because they're very, very old. They could die naturally because they're very, very sick. Dying of an illness such as heart disease or cancer is called a natural cause of death. You may hear someone say, "The cause of death was a sudden heart attack."

Some people are sick for a long, long time. Others die when no one is even thinking about their dying. This is called SUDDEN DEATH.

Some people kill themselves. That is a sudden death. That is called SUICIDE (sue-a-side). You may hear people say, "He took his own life," or "He completed suicide." That was the cause of death. Other people say, "She suicided."

When one person kills another person, the cause of death is called a HOMICIDE (hom-a-side) or murder. Some sudden deaths are caused by ACCIDENTS (axe-a-dents).

DISASTERS (dis-ass-ters) can also be a cause of death. There are weather disasters such as hurricanes, tornados or earthquakes. There are disasters caused by people, such as war or terrorism. Usually with a disaster, several people die at once. You may hear someone say, "The hurricane was a terrible disaster."

Sometimes when a person dies suddenly, it can be hard for doctors to say what caused the person to die, but usually we can find the cause of death. Everything and everyone who lives will have a lifetime and finally, a cause of death.

When the chemo stopped working and the radiation stopped working we lost Paige.
That's what my grandma said, "lost." My parents said she died. I couldn't say anything at all.

Lost and Found by Ellen Yeomans

Cemetery

Say it: SEM-a-tare-ee

A special place where the bodies of people who have died are buried in the ground.

You may hear someone say, "The cemetery is so beautiful at sunset, and the sun shines on his grave every afternoon."

Years ago, cemeteries were next to churches and were called GRAVEYARDS (GUR-ave-yards). In some places these are called BURIAL GROUNDS (bear–ee-all-grounds). Some cemeteries are still owned by churches, and if you drive through the country or live in a small town you will probably see a quiet graveyard by a church.

Many cemeteries are called MEMORIAL PARKS (mem-or-ee-all) or MEMORIAL GARDENS. The land is usually very nice, with green grass, bushes and flowers.

A BURIAL PLOT (bear-ee-al Pa-lot) or GRAVESITE (Gr-ave-site) is the place where the body is buried. Families often bring flowers to the gravesite and there is usually a headstone there. The HEADSTONE (HED-st-own) or MARKER tells the name of the person's body buried in the grave. It also tells the year the person was born and the year the person died.

The grave is carefully filled with the earth that was dug so the casket could go into the ground After awhile, the earth over the grave is smooth and covered with grass. The grave becomes a part of the cemetery.

Our center for grieving children meets in a funeral home building beside the cemetery. My mom is buried there. After the meeting, my dad and I walk up to her grave and say hello.
We know she can't hear us, but we think maybe her spirit does. The cemetery is like being out in nature and even when there's snow on the ground, it's a nice place to visit. Sometimes we stop at the grocery store before the meeting and get a little bouquet of flowers to put on her grave.

Antonio, age 11

Center for Grieving Children

A special place for children who have a death in the family.

You may hear someone say, "All the kids like to go to The Warm Place. It is a center for grieving children."

There are many ways centers for grieving children help a child after a death. There are groups of children your age. Everyone in the group has had a family member or someone they love who has died. There are special activities to help you remember your person. There are groups for parents and other family members, too.

A center for grieving children is a safe place to talk about your loved one who died. There are a lot of kids there, and they all understand what it's like to be sad.

To find a center near you, go with a parent on the internet and type in www.Dougy.org. The Dougy Center is the oldest center for grieving children in the country. They have a list of other centers all over the United States. If there is a center near you, maybe your family can take you. It can be very helpful.

Story:
When my grandmother died, my mom took me to Ted E. Bear Hollow in Omaha, Nebraska. Ted E. Bear Hollow is a special place where kids go after someone in their family dies. We had pizza with a lot of other families, then we all had different groups.

My group had seven kids in it. One kid's mother had died, another kid's uncle died – there were all kinds of deaths. We could talk and no one got worried that we were talking about our people who died. It was really neat. I went for a bunch of weeks, then I didn't think I needed to go any more, but I know I can always go back if I want to.

Kelly, age 8

Columbarium

Say it: Kol-um-BEAR-ee-um

You may hear someone say, "We'll go to the columbarium where your grandmother's ashes are and leave some flowers there. We'll take flowers she loved when she was alive."

A special room where the ashes are kept after a body has been cremated. Some columbariums have beautiful art and stained glass windows. Others are very simple and plain.

Each columbarium has a space to hold one URN (err-n) or jar, holding the ashes. That space is called a NICHE (Neh-itch).

Story:
Children and adults have loved reading James Barrie's *Peter Pan*. Movies have been made about it. One was *Finding Neverland*, the story of how Mr. Barrie came to write the book. Had Scottish-born James had a "normal" childhood, there might never have been a Peter Pan. James was the ninth of ten children. He heard stories of pirates from his mother, who read stories from Robert Lewis Stevenson to her children at night. When James was seven, his brother, who was their mother's "favorite son" died in a skating accident. To comfort his mother, James dressed up in his brother's clothes. His mother was shocked and he felt terrible. He was only trying to help. His mother never talked about it, but he knew his plan to help hadn't worked. He felt like a "lost boy," forced to grow up to soon. Friends thought James never grew up, just like Peter Pan. *Finding Neverland* is a wonderful story for and about grieving children.

Committal

Say it: Kum-MIT-all

Placing the casket in the GRAVE (grr-ave) or BURIAL PLOT (bear-ee-all pa-lot) or in the MAUSOLEUM (maw-so-lee-um).

You may hear someone say, "After the committal, we're going back to the church for lunch."

From ancient times this service has been called a committal because the soul was committed to God and the body committed to the earth.

Often a minister, rabbi, priest or close family friend reads some words or says things to comfort the family and friends gathered at the grave following the funeral.

In some religions, family members shovel some of the earth onto the casket. Sometimes people take some of the earth in their hands and throw it gently on top of the casket. This was a way of showing that death was final. People may also feel a closer part of the BURIAL (bear-ee-all) when this is done. Some family members and friends leave the cemetery right away. Others stay and visit with relatives and friends. Some may watch the casket lowered into the grave.

Not all committal means saying goodbye to the body by placing it in a grave or mausoleum. Listen to these beautiful words from a Native American story:

> *They took her away from the camp along a creek and put her on a platform*
> *among the branches of an old cottonwood tree.*
> *The earth would soon take back her body*
> *and her spirit would be free in the winds and clouds.*

Beyond the Ridge by Paul Goble

24

Condolence

Say it: Kun-DOE-lence

Telling a grieving person you are sad about what happened.
It is a very old word meaning, giving comfort.

You may hear someone say, "I am so sorry for your loss."
That is a condolence.

Many people come to the funeral home to see the family and offer condolences.
When people walk up to the grieving person, shake her hand or give her a hug that is offering condolences.

Some people send cards or emails or call on the phone. Often they stop by the house. Often they bring food for the family and all the people coming from out of town.

After someone dies, the family knows there is nothing to say that will take the sad away, but they are happy people have come to see them and offer condolences.

Sometimes this is called, PAYING RESPECTS (pa-ing ree-speks).

A part of offering condolences is promising and giving future help. After his neighbor Mr. Vernon died, Karl, age 12, helped Mrs. Vernon pull weeds in the garden. "I can help you do this every week, Mrs. Vernon," he promised. And all summer, he helped pull the weeds and they talked. After the work, Mrs. Vernon served Karl monster cookies. "You're my most helpful neighbor, Karl," she told him.

The house was bursting at the seams with people who loved my daddy.
No one came empty-handed, either.
There were people from our church, from Daddy's work and even from his barbershop.
They brought cakes, flowers, and macaroni and yes, some fried chicken.

Sunflowers and Rainbows for Tia by Alesia Alexander Greene

Cremation

Say it: Kree-MAY-shun

A way of turning a dead body into a soft ash.

You may hear someone say, "My granddad always told us he wanted his body cremated."

The body is taken very carefully to a special room. This is not like any room you have in your house. There is a special heat in this tiny room, not like any heat in a fireplace or in a furnace. This heat is so hot it slowly dissolves the body.

When the cremation is finished, what is left of the body is a soft ash. The person caring for the body gently collects the ashes. The ashes are put into a special machine. The machine makes them even smaller. Now the ashes really look like ground-up seashells or very coarse or chunky sand.

This is done in a place called a CREMATORY (KREE-mah-tor-ee) or CREMATOIUM (kree-MAH-tor-ee-um). These places are made just to turn bodies into ash.

The ashes are placed in a jar called an URN (err-n). The ashes are called CREMAINS (kree-may-ns) or CREMATED REMAINS (kree-MAY-ted re-may-ns).

Remember, when people are dead, they can't feel anything. They cannot feel the heat.

We have had cremation for thousands of years. Today, more and more people are choosing cremation. All bodies finally return to the good earth. Cremation is just one way to make that happen faster.

Your family will have a special place for the urn and the ashes.
Maybe you can see the urn and ask more questions.
Your family can do many very nice things with the ashes.
Some people scatter the ashes over a favorite place.
Some people bury the urn or keep it in a special place at the cemetery.
Some people keep a tiny bit of the ashes in a locket or in a tiny box.

Tell Me, Papa by Joy and Dr. Marvin Johnson

26

Day of the Dead

Say it: Daa of the Ded

People of Mexican tradition celebrate their dead family members on November 1st and 2nd.

You may hear someone say, "My friend Juan invited me to his house on Day of the Dead."

Because of their understanding of death, this day is not sad. Children enjoy toys or candy made in the shape of skeletons. Bright orange marigold flowers are used for decorations in homes. Families meet at the grave to talk and remember their loved ones. Many believe the dead return for a special visit on these nights following HALLOWEEN. One special activity on the Day of the Dead is eating PAN DE METRO (the bread of death). The bread is shaped like human beings, alligators, skulls and crossbones. Many families build small altars in their homes and place special things such as pictures or belongings or objects the people who died liked, such as their favorite candies.

On our Halloween, people dress up as GHOSTS and monsters. Ghosts come from stories of people whose spirits return or stay on earth. Ghost stories are what one boy called, "A fun way to be scared and safe at the same time."

One religion, called Shinto also honors the dead. O-BON is that religion's festival of the dead. People believe the souls of their ancestors briefly return to earth. Families cook special food the ancestors enjoyed and light farewell torches so they can find the path back.

Some Christian churches celebrate the Day of the Dead, too. During the church service, candles are lit and the names of people who died are read.

*Some cultures believe the Soul of a dead person
will stay near his or her home
and that the dead person's family can talk to the Soul, like in a dream,
asking the Soul for help with problems,
like a sickness in the family or not having enough food to eat.*

What is Death? by Etan Boritzer

Dead

Say it: Ded

When a person's body no longer works, that person is dead. All that is left is the body. The life in that person; the laughter, the tears, the feelings – the tasting, moving, eating, going to the bathroom – the thinking and talking – are gone. The body is like a peanut shell with no peanut, an egg shell with no egg inside, a school with no children.

Sometimes people say the dead person has, "passed away." Sometimes people say the dead person has "passed," or "gone." But remember, dead is dead. It's not like we passed a test or are gone from a room.

Sometimes the word, DEAD can be confusing, but it always means "not working or not there."
"My cell phone is dead."
"There was dead silence in the room."
"This town is really dead in the winter."

The cell phone can be made to work again, and someone in the room will say something to break the silence, and when winter is gone the town will come to life again. It's different for people and animals. After someone dies, they never come to life again, even if you've seen that happen in movies or TV and in cartoons.

Sometimes it's hard to believe a person is really dead, especially if we loved that person a lot.

What does dead mean?
When someone dies, her body stops working.
The heart stops beating, and breathing stops.
The brain doesn't send or receive messages.
She no longer can see, hear, touch, taste, smell, eat, play, feel or think. She cannot move.
Someone dead may look asleep, but she isn't sleeping and she cannot wake up.

When Dinosaurs Die by Laurie Krasny Brown and Marc Brown

Death

Say it: Deth

The end of life.

A person who has died, has experienced death.

You may hear someone say, "His death was very sudden."

Birth and death are like two bookends – the beginning and the end, with life in between.

Death is a natural part of life.

*There is a beginning and an ending
for everything that is alive.
In between is living.
Nothing that is alive goes on living forever.
How long it lives depends upon what it is and
what happens while it is living.*

*So, no matter how long they are,
or how short, lifetimes are really all the same.
They have a beginning and an ending,
and there is living in between.*

Lifetimes by Bryan Mellonie and Robert Ingpen

29

Death Certificate

Say it: Deth Cer-TIF-a-cut

An important paper from the government that says when, where, and how a person died. The courts and banks and insurance companies know the person died when they see the death certificate.

You may hear someone say, "What was the cause of death listed on the death certificate?"

Your birth was recorded with an important piece of paper called a BIRTH CERTIFICATE. **Your death will be recorded by an important piece of paper called a DEATH CERTIFICATE.**

Story: When I went through my Aunt Ada's things after her funeral, I found treasures:
Beautiful rings,
Pins,
Quilt tops,
Photos – some fifty years old.
And the important papers of her life –
Her Sunday school attendance record,
Her baptism certificate,
Her award for the best cookies in a cooking contest,
Her birth certificate,
Her marriage license.
When we got her death certificate, I put all those pieces of paper – old and new – in a plastic envelope along with her photo. It was a gentle record of her life and death.

Aunt Ada Died by Joy Johnson

Deceased

Say it: Dee-ceesed

Another word for the person who has died.

You may hear someone say, "The deceased will be at the Smith Funeral Home."

Usually the person who died is called, THE DECEASED.

Some people are not comfortable with death and may talk about THE BODY. Sometimes the person who died is called THE LOVED ONE.

Deceased means dead. The very earliest word, hundreds of years ago, was deces, which simply meant dead.

Story: Before the funeral, the funeral director called my uncle, "The Deceased." I sat with the other kids, and we started whispering, saying – "Deee seeeeeeest." And making snake sounds. We thought it was the funniest word we'd ever heard, and we knew our uncle would be there hissing it the loudest of all if he was alive. He loved funny things.

Jennifer, age 10, from a support group for grieving children

Disaster

Say it: Dis-ASS-ter

A tragedy where many people die.

You may hear someone say, "That war was a real disaster."

A NATURAL (nat-jur-all) DISASTER is a tornado, hurricane, earthquake or flood. Hurricane Katrina killed over 1,000 people in Louisiana, Missippi and Florida. The largest natural disaster in ten years.

A MAN-MADE DISASTER is one where people kill people.

When planes hit the World Trade Center a few years ago; that was a TERRORIST (Ter-or-ist) DISASTER.

Story: I think a disaster is just when something really, really bad happens. My mom died in the car wreck, and over and over my sister keeps saying, "That was such a disaster for us." Disaster comes in all sizes, from my mom's dying to my getting a bad grade on a test. Sometimes, I just have a bad day and I say, "Today was a disaster!"

Janet at KidsKamp for grieving children

Donation (Body or Organ)

Say it: Doe-NA-shun

There are two kinds of donations when someone dies:
    Body Donation
    Organ Donation

You may hear someone say, "He went to Omaha for a kidney transplant." Or, "My brother's heart and liver were donated to kids who wouldn't have lived without them."

With a body donation, instead of being buried or cremated, the body is given to a medical school so young people studying to become doctors can learn all about the body and all the different parts. When this happens, the body has a special name. It's called a CADAVER (kah-DAV-er). Some people say they want to do this because even after death, they can help another person. Their bodies can help doctors learn. After the body has been studied, it is CREMATED (go to the page talking about CREMATION) and the ashes returned to the family.

In an organ donation, parts of the body are taken out by doctors right after the person has died. These parts, or organs, go very quickly to people waiting for a TRANSPLANT (trans-pah-lant). A special container holds the organ while it travels to the sick person who needs it. As soon as it gets to the sick person, other doctors do surgery and put the organ of the person who died into the living person waiting for it.

While we are sad when someone we love dies, we can feel good if they were an organ donor and other people have new life because a part of our person helped them live.

I just knew the heart Gracie got had to come from a special person.
Grandpa Marty in the movie ***Return to Me***

Euphemisms

Say it: YOU-fem-ism

A very big word that means using pleasant or nice words for something you may think is painful or that people won't like.

You may hear someone say, "We lost Grandpa last month." It still means Grandpa is dead. It's a way of saying we have lost the love and comfort and the person who was our grandpa.

People use euphemisms when they try to make death less painful. They use words they think will be less harsh or hurtful.

There is an old poem that says, "He is not dead, just gone away." Others say, "He passed away." Some say, "She looks so peaceful." "She looks like she's asleep." Dead bodies may look peaceful or look as if they're asleep, but they are dead.

Some euphemisms seem funny:
"He kicked the bucket."
"He bought the farm," or
"He cashed in his chips."

Some people use euphemisms because they don't know what to say. It's often better just to say, "I don't know what to say."

The important thing to remember is that the person is dead, not asleep. They haven't "passed" as they could pass you on the street when they were alive. "Passed" is a word often used by church people to mean the dead have "passed" from this life into the next. It's part of their beliefs and important to them.

Then a very tall lady bent over me. "I'm sorry you lost your Grandpa," she said.
"It's always sad when Grandpas die."
Die! My grandpa was dead? I began to understand. "Lost" was a grown-up word for die.

Finding Grandpa Everywhere by John Hodge

Family Car

Say it: Fam-il-ee Kar

A special car in which family members ride together to the funeral home, church or cemetery. Sometimes the family car is a very long one called a LIMOUSINE (Lim-O-seen).

You may hear someone say, "Six of us rode in the family car."

The funeral home uses the family car so members of the family can be together. In the family car, someone from the funeral home is driving so everyone in the family can be together and not be bothered by traffic. The family car usually follows the HEARSE (herse) or COACH in the funeral procession.

Only close relatives of the dead person ride in the family car. These people can be the wife or husband, the son or daughter, grandchildren or others chosen by the family. Most people drive their own cars to the cemetery, following the hearse and the family car.

Story: It was the biggest car I had ever been in. All eight of us could sit in it. We could even face each other. Mostly it was my cousins, but my mom and dad and Aunt Jen and Uncle Tom were there, too. Uncle Tom talked about where he would go if he owned a car like the family car. We started laughing and it felt good. It was a really nice ride to the cemetery.

Larissa, age 9

Fear or Afraid

Say it: **Fere** and **A-frade**

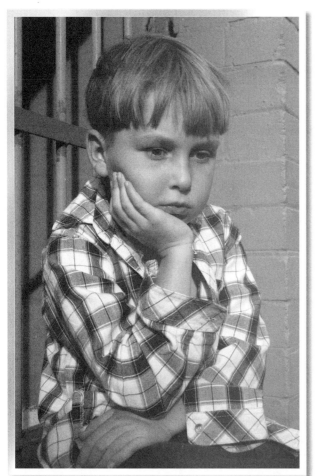

You may hear someone say, "I was afraid someone else would die, too."

Fear is what you feel when you are scared or frightened of something. It's one of the feelings that often comes after someone dies. After someone dies, a lot of things change. That can be very scary. What you need to know is that it's okay to be afraid after someone dies, just like it's okay to be sad and angry and confused.

Remember, it won't last forever. For a while you may be afraid someone else will die. You may be afraid when you don't know what will happen next. You may be afraid just before you go to the funeral because it's all different. You may be afraid of meeting so many new people.

Things won't be the same again. Someone you love has died. But you and your family will create a new normal.

That's a fear a lot of young people like you have. It hardly ever happens at all. You'll always have someone to love and care for you.

I'm more scared now than I used to be. I don't want to be by myself. I keep the lights on at night. I tell my folks when I'm scared and that helps.

Since My Brother Died by Marisol Munoz-Kiehne

Feelings

Say it: Fee-lings

All the ups and downs we feel inside when someone we love dies. There are so many feelings we can't put them all on one page.

You may hear someone say, "You seem to be coping very well since your father's death."

Feelings are also called EMOTIONS (Ee-mow-shuns). What we do with our feelings or emotions is called COPING (Kope-ing). We cope. Some people cope by working hard. Some people cope by talking about their feelings. Some people cope by reading books on grief. There are a lot of ways to cope.

Sometimes, when things get very emotional and difficult, we have what is called a CRISIS(cry-sis). A crisis is when something very hard and difficult happens to us. A long illness can be a crisis. When the illness becomes much worse very fast, that can be a crisis. A sudden death may be a crisis, too. Crisis also happens when a family doesn't have enough money or insurance. A national disaster can be a disaster like hurricanes or war.

You may hear someone say, "My dad's death is the biggest crisis this family has ever faced."

Story: When my sister died, I had more feelings and emotions than I ever thought I could have. When I was with my school counselor, she asked me to list my feelings and this is what I put down: SAD!, Mad!!, Lost. Alone. Afraid. Hurt. Bummed Out. Confused. And a lot, lot more, too. My counselor said we should add "Denial" – that means pretending it didn't happen. Sometimes I have to do that – deny it; pretend it didn't happen. But it doesn't last very long. I always remember.

Kara, age 11

Funeral Director

Say it: FEW-ner-all Dur-ECT-er

A man or woman who works at the funeral home and does a special job. They go to a special school to learn how to do this job.

You may hear someone say, "The funeral director was very helpful to our family."

Funeral directors take care of the body of the person who died. They help the family plan the funeral or memorial service.

Sometimes funeral directors are called, UNDERTAKERS. This comes from them "undertaking" the task of burying the body. Sometimes funeral directors are called, MORTICIANS (more-TISH-ans). This comes from the Latin word, mortis or MORTUARY (MORTCH-u -air-ee). Mortuary is another word for the funeral home.

Like a lot of grown-ups, funeral directors may be moms and dads. Most of them have children and families of their own.

They help families who are grieving, too. If you want, you can meet the funeral director caring for your family. Ask for his or her name and tell the director your name, too.

There is nothing a funeral director does that cannot be explained lovingly and caringly to children.
Thank You For Coming To Say Goodbye by Janice Roberts

Funeral Home

Say it: FEW-ner-all Hom

The special building where the body of the person who died is taken after death.

Funeral homes come in all shapes and sizes. Most of them look like very big, comfortable houses. Even the ones that are more like office buildings, look like houses when you get inside.

They're comfortable. They have nice furniture. There are people there who will care for you and your family.

There will be a room with a big table or desk and comfortable chairs. That is where your family will decide what to do at the funeral. They will talk with a FUNERAL DIRECTOR. You will probably be offered something to drink like coffee for grown-ups and juice for you.

Another room in the funeral home is filled with CASKETS. You may get to go into this room and look at all the different kinds of caskets.

Another room in the funeral home is called the PREPARATION ROOM. This is where the funeral directors very carefully wash the dead person's body. This is the room where the body is EMBALMED (m-balmed). When a body is embalmed, all the blood is carefully drained out of the body. A special liquid is put into the veins so the body will look pinker and will last longer. It is called EMBALMING FLUID.

The funeral home may be a very busy place. It is where you will go for your person's VISITATION or CALLING HOURS. That is the time when family and friends come together to visit before the FUNERAL. Many times the funeral or memorial service will be held in the funeral home.

Story: The funeral home was a really big house with a nice porch all around it. We went there for my grandfather's funeral. When my uncle died, the funeral home was all brick and square but it has a porch on the front. What I liked best about it was a play area inside. I took my little brother there and he enjoyed the toys and books. Some books showed pictures of funeral homes and that was cool.

Kerisha, age 12

Funeral Meal

Say it: Few-ner-all Meel

You may hear, "I thought I couldn't eat, but once I got there, everything was good and people talked and laughed and remembered my aunt."

Fixing food for grieving families goes back a long, long time. Friends bring casseroles, salads and desserts and other things good to eat. Fixing food helps the family and lets people know they are doing something to help.

Often the church or funeral home holds a funeral meal or funeral lunch before or after the service. This meal is usually only for the family and close friends.

There are good things to eat. Some people call foods they really like, COMFORT FOODS. A lot of people list things like brownies and ice cream as their comfort foods.

Sometimes people have snacks or a meal for everyone attending the service. One lady told her family she wanted to have an ice cream social after her funeral. They did, with lots and lots of ice cream and cake for everyone.

Usually funeral meals start slowly and quietly while people gather. Soon, though, there is talk and laughter and people feel good about being together, even though this is may be a sad time.

Story: *Johnny's Funeral*

We were all young adults when our friend, Johnny, died. His funeral was in a tiny church several miles from where we lived. He was buried in the little cemetery by the church. Afterwards, we all went into the church for a big lunch cooked by the church ladies. I thought, "How can people laugh and have fun during this sad time?" Soon I found out how very healing and comforting a funeral meal and laughter could be.

Joy Johnson

Funeral Procession

Say it: Few-ner-all Pro-shess-shun

The long line of cars that follows the funeral coach or hearse that is carrying the body.
It's like a long, sad, slow parade to the cemetery.

You may hear someone say, "That is a very long funeral procession."

In ancient times the body was carried to the cemetery in a carriage drawn by horses. People walked behind the horses carrying torches. This was a torch-light procession. Even today, cars in a funeral procession have their lights on. This also lets people know those cars are in a special procession, going to the cemetery.

Some funeral homes put small flags on the cars so other drivers know it's a funeral procession. A MOTORCYCLE ESCORT (moe-tor-sigh-cul S-cort) leads some funeral processions. Special procession cars lead other funeral processions. The cars go ahead of the procession and stop traffic at stoplights so the procession can pass through the intersection without stopping.

When United States Presidents die, people line the streets to stand quietly while the funeral procession goes by.

When the funeral ends, pallbearers – often friends of the family - may carry the casket to the hearse or funeral coach. Close relatives may ride in special cars. Other people follow the hearse and limousines in their own cars. This is called the funeral procession. It is the quiet parade to the cemetery where your person will be buried.

A *Child's Book About Funerals and Cemeteries* by Earl Grollman and Joy Johnson

Funeral Service

Say it: FEW-ner-all

A special time after a person has died when family, friends and neighbors come together to say goodbye and offer condolences.

You may hear someone say, "The funeral was really beautiful." "That memorial service was a real celebration of my aunt's life."

Sometimes the funeral is in the funeral home. The funeral home is where the body was taken after the person died. Sometimes the funeral is in the CHURCH or SYNAGOGUE (SIN-a-gog). It's a time to remember the person; to say goodbye and thank you to the person who lived. There will be music and sometimes songs and prayers.

Usually someone will speak. What that person says about the person who died is called a EULOGY(YOU-ol-gee). Sometimes several people talk about the person who died. They share memories and good times they had with the person who died. They tell about that person's life.

The body is always present at a funeral. Maybe the casket will be open; maybe it will be closed.

If the body is not present, the service is called a MEMORIAL SERVICE (mem-OR-ee-all ser-vis).

Some funerals and memorial services are like being in church or at temple. A minister, priest or rabbi will say prayers. These friends are called CLERGY (Klerg-ee). If you are Jewish, your clergy person will be a Rabbi. If you are Catholic or Episcopalian or Orthodox, your clergy will be a Priest. If you are Muslim, your clergy will be an Emir.

Some services can be very short and others can be very long. Some families like to call the funeral or memorial service a CELEBRATION OF LIFE (sell-a-BRAY-shun). That means we share how grateful we are that our person lived. We are happy for their life and time with us.

Grave and Graveyard

Say it: Grr-ave and Grr-ave-yard)

The grave is a special hole, carefully dug in the CEMETERY (SEM-a-tare-ee). This hole is called the grave.

You may hear someone say, "Would you like to go put some flowers on Grandpa's grave?"

The vault is in the grave to protect the casket and the body inside. The casket holding the body goes into the vault. After the body and casket are inside the vault, the hole is filled in and you have a grave. That special place in the cemetery is your loved one's GRAVESITE (Gur-ave-cite).

For a while the dirt on top of the grave is higher than the earth around it. It forms a little mound. Gradually this dirt settles around the vault and the ground becomes level. Often flowers from the funeral are placed on top of the grave.

The beautiful land filled with graves is called a GRAVEYARD. It's an old name for a cemetery.

Not all bodies are buried in graveyards.

President Ronald Reagan's body was buried at his presidential library in California. Princess Diana's body was buried on an island on her family's property. John F. Kennedy Jr., the son of President Kennedy, was buried at sea.

Some people say goodbye by putting some of the tender earth into the grave.
Others take a flower from on or near the casket.
Finally, the casket will be covered with the good, rich earth dug just for it.
It will stay there and be safe.

Tell Me, Papa by Joy and Dr. Marvin Johnson

43

Grief

Say it: Greef

All the feelings that come after someone you love dies.

You may hear someone say, "How long will this grief last?"

We all have a lot of feelings when a person dies. People who love that person may feel:

    Sad
    Mad
    Lonely
    Relieved if the person was very, very sick
    Hurt
    Tired

When people have grief, we say they are grieving. Grief can last a long, long time.

No matter how long your grief lasts, you never forget the person who died. Sometimes years later, you remember something about that person and feel sad all over again.

Grief comes at times when no one dies. Grief comes whenever you lose someone or something important to you. People you love get a divorce and you grieve. When a pet dies, you grieve. When you move to a new house and you miss your old home, you grieve. When someone hurts your feelings, you have a little grief.

There are big griefs and little griefs. They are all a part of life. They all bring a lot of feelings. It's important to learn to share your feelings with someone you trust. It's important that you know grief is normal and okay. Grief often brings tears, and crying is okay, too. In fact, crying can be good for you. Crying can help you feel better.

Mamita died one day while I was at school. I had painted her a big orange sun that day. I did not feel very sunny when I heard about Mamita. I was so sad, I tore up my beautiful sun.

A Mural for Mamita by Alesia Alexander

Grief Group

Say it: Greef Groop

A special gathering of people who are grieving.

You may hear, "My grief group is a safe place. I don't have to pretend I feel okay."

Some grief groups are led by people who get special training on how to be a group leader. Some grief groups are led by people whose loved one has died some time ago. The group leader starts the talking and makes sure the people in the group all have a chance to talk and listen to each other. People share their feelings and what they have learned from their grief. They share ways to help each other and say what works for them to help them feel better. People in grief groups share stories of their loved one who died. They laugh. They cry sometimes, too. They can become very close friends. They all understand each other and know how the other people feel.

Most grief groups are called SUPPORT GROUPS (Supp-ort Groops). (See BEREAVEMENT SUPPORT GROUP). People in the group care for each other. To support another person means you listen to them; you don't tell them how to think or feel, and become a friend to them. If you are crying and someone who cares puts an arm around you, that is supporting you.

There are support groups for grown-ups and for kids, too.

Story: Alejandro wore his daddy's lab coat to Ted E. Bear Hollow, our center for grieving children. He told his group how his father had died. His daddy had been a doctor and Alejandro knew his grief group would listen to his story. He knew they would understand.

Sarah, Ted E. Bear Hollow group leader

45

Guilt or Guilty

Say it: Gilt

A feeling you've done something wrong.

You may hear someone say, "My mom feels guilty because she had to stay at home and work and couldn't go to Florida until just before my grandfather died. She wanted to spend more time with him."

Some people think they should have done more to help a sick person. They feel guilty. Some people wish they had told a person how they loved her before she died. They feel guilty. Some people get angry at others in their family after the death. They feel guilty.

What is really important is to know you don't need to feel guilty about your person's death. Nothing you did or said made them sick or made them have an accident or made them die. You did not do anything wrong! It was not your fault the person you loved died.

One boy felt guilty that he didn't go to his grandfather's room to say goodbye before he died. He was sorry.

When we feel sorry or guilty about something like that, there are other things we can do to help. Even though his grandfather was dead, the boy wrote a goodbye letter to him and put it in Grandfather's casket before the funeral.

He knew his grandfather would understand. The boy was afraid. He was just a little boy. He did the best he could at the time, and he made up for it afterward.

> *My mom said nothing I did made Jess die.*
> *She said nothing I did made Jess sick, either.*
> *Mom said nothing I can say can make her cry.*
> *I can talk about Jess all I want to.*
> *I can ask questions.*
> *She says if she cries, that is good. Crying gets her sad out.*
> *We can cry together because we love Jess and we miss her.*

Where's Jess? by Ray, Jody and Heather Goldstein

Headstone

Say it: HED-stone

You may hear someone say, "We're going to pick out a headstone for the grave."

It has always been important to mark a grave so everyone can know who is buried there. In pioneer days, when wagon trains crossed the prairies, if someone died stones were piled on the grave to mark that place.

Headstones get their name because they are very nice, large, carefully carved pieces of stone. They are placed at the head of the grave. The body lays buried in the grave and the stone is placed above the head. The stone faces the feet of the dead person who is buried underneath the soft earth.

The headstone may also be called a MARKER (mar-ker). Older people may call it a TOMBSTONE (toom-stone). At one time graves were often called tombs (tooms). Whatever it is called, the stone or marker:

> Tells the person's name.
> Tells the date they were born and the date they died.
> Reminds us how special they were.

Headstones also help us find the graves of people when we want to take flowers or just go see the grave.

In older cemeteries, you may see MONUMENTS (mon-u-ments). These are really large markers that may just have the family's name on them.

Cemeteries can be very beautiful and interesting. You may see statues of angels or important people. You'll often see special symbol or pictures on some of the headstones or monuments. When a baby died, sometimes a little lamb was carved into the headstone, or a statue of a lamb rested on top of the stone. Some headstones have special sayings from the Bible carved into them. Some headstones say who that person was and what they meant to the family, such as; Our Mother, or Beloved Husband.

If you have visited a cemetery, maybe you can draw pictures of the statues and headstones you've seen there.

Hearse or Coach

Say it: Herse

A big, special car used to carry the dead body in the casket to the cemetery.

You may hear someone say, "The hearse moved very slowly."

A hearse was once a special, beautiful wagon pulled by horses. A long time ago, people turned a farm plow or and placed the casket on it and called it a herse. Some people think the first person who did this pronounced horse as herse and that's how it got its name.

Another name for the hearse is COACH (ca-oh-ch). Today more people call the big, special car a funeral coach. Coach is a word that is very old, too. The fancy wagons drawn by horses to carry important people were coaches. Now the funeral coach will carry the body of your important person who has died.

Hearses or funeral coaches come in different colors. Many are black. Some are white. Some are grey. Some are even green.

Often the name of the funeral home is written on the inside of the window. The hearse leads the funeral procession in the long parade to the cemetery.

Sometimes a special car with flashing lights goes in front of the funeral coach to stop traffic and let the funeral procession pass safely through the intersections. Sometimes a motorcycle escort travels in front of the coach to make sure it's safe.

When his friends lifted the casket into the hearse, I said, "There goes our daddy," and my sister and I cried. Then we followed the hearse all the way to the cemetery.

Rachael, age 13

Homicide

Say it: HOM-a-side

When a person kills another person on purpose.

You may hear someone say, "The police think the death was a homicide."

Sometimes a person doesn't think right. They become sick in their mind. That person's mind doesn't work as it should. When that happens, sometimes that person kills another person. When this happens it makes us very mad and sad.

Homicide is a big word for MURDER (MER-der). Usually, the person who does the killing is caught and sent to jail. Sometimes, though, this doesn't happen. This can mean the family's grief lasts a lot longer.

You may hear another word for homicide. You may hear MANSLAUGHTER (MAN-slaw-ter). Manslaughter happens when a person kills someone during a fight or without thinking about it. Homicide happens when a murder is planned ahead of time. You may hear about pre-meditated murder. That means the killing has been planned.

There is motor vehicle homicide where someone who may be drunk hits a car and someone dies. There is justifiable homicide where a soldier or policeman kills a enemy or criminal. No matter how it happens, all the families are very, very sad. Even the family of the person who did the killing suffers and grieves.

Another kind of homicide happens when someone kills more than one person. This is known as TERRORISM (TER-or-ism).

No matter how it happens, homicide brings many feelings:
>Anger
>Sadness
>Fear
>Unsafe

Story: *I remember more than anything, the coffins. The small coffins. And the sense that Birmingham wasn't a very safe place.*

Condoleezza Rice remembering the murder of her friend, Denise McNair in the bombing of Sixteenth Avenue Baptist Church in 1963. Condoleezza Rice was Secretary of State in 2005.

49

Hospice

Say it: HOSS-pus

A program that helps care for people who are dying and for their families.

You may hear someone say, "The hospice people did so much to help us. They were like a really loving family."

Doctors and nurses do everything they can to help a person get well. Sometimes, no matter what they do, the person does not get better. Everyone knows the person is going to die soon. When that happens, the family can call a hospice.

Hospices help the dying person die at home or in a home-like place instead of the hospital. Hospices make sure the dying person is comfortable and not hurting. They care for the family and help them get ready for the death. Very often, the person dies very quietly and comfortably.

One morning Mother stopped Megan as she walked into Grandmother's house with her bouquet of lilacs. "Grandma's gone, Megan. She died very quietly and peacefully this morning." Megan buried her head in the bouquet and cried.

Lilacs for Grandma by Margene Hucek

Infant Death, Stillbirth, Sudden Infant Death

Say it: Still-berth

When a baby is born and is not alive, that is called a stillbirth.

You may hear someone say, "It was such a surprise. The baby was born dead."

A lot of times, we don't know why this happens, it just does. Other times the baby wasn't strong like you were when you were born. Sometimes, big kids like you wonder if something they did made the baby die. That's not true. Nothing you did or thought could make a baby die. The baby just couldn't live outside Mommy's tummy for some reason.

Sudden Infant Death Syndrome /SIDS

Say it: Sud-n In-fant and Deth Sin-drom

When young babies die unexpectedly in their sleep it's called Sudden Infant Death or SIDS.
It doesn't happen because of anything anybody did or did not do.

You may hear someone say, "This is so sad. Such a sweet happy baby and now he's dead."

For a long time doctors all over the world have tried to figure out what parents and others can do to stop SIDS.

SIDS is different than STILLBIRTH. In Stillbirth the baby dies when she is born or just before. In Sudden Infant Death Syndrome, the baby can be several months old.

If the baby is going to be buried, often big brothers and sisters put a special toy or stuffed animal or a picture they've drawn in the baby's casket.

This was a real baby, with a real name and a real family. Even if we don't have a lot of memories of babies who die, they're a part of our family. It's good to remember them during holidays like Christmas or Hanukkah or Kwanzaa.

When a baby dies, everyone has a lot of questions. All your questions are okay.

51

Lost or Loss

Say it: Lawst

This is how some people talk about the person who died.

You may hear someone say, "He lost his grandfather this year."

It's also a euphemism (You-fem-ism) – or a word we use when we want to soften what we're saying or make it less painful.

People whose loved one has died are said to have suffered a loss. If you've ever watched a police show on television or in the movies, you may have heard a policeman or woman tell a family member, "I'm sorry for your loss," after someone has been killed on the show.

The word, lost can be confusing for kids. When we lose something, we look for it until we find it. When someone has died, we can't find them alive again.

There are things we CAN find, though. We can find good memories and happy memories. We can find things inside us they have taught us. We can find ways we're like them – how we look, how we act. So people who die aren't really lost to us in our hearts and memories.

Mom said Grandma lost Grandpa.
I wondered how anyone as big as Grandpa could be lost.
There were a lot of people at Grandma's house.
They must be the search party going out to find Grandpa.
They were dressed really nice to go searching
and they were eating a lot.
They must need to eat and keep their strength up
for the search.

Finding Grandpa Everywhere by John Hodge

Mausoleum

Say it: Maw-so-LEE-um

A special place, usually in a cemetery, where bodies are kept.

You may hear someone say, "That big building at the center of the cemetery is a mausoleum."

If a body has been cremated, the cremated remains can be kept in a mausoleum, too. This means the body is not buried under the ground, even though we talk about people being buried when the body is carefully kept in this special building or place.

In some parts of the country, where cities are close to the ocean, there are several mausoleums. That is because the city is so close to sea level that water can seep into graves under the ground. Some of the oldest and most beautiful are in New Orleans, Louisiana.

In other parts of the country, where land is very expensive, there are more mausoleums because many caskets or urns can be placed close together.

Story: Every year on Memorial Day the oldest cemetery in our city has a program.
People dress up in pioneer clothes and stand by the graves of the pioneers who died 100 years ago or even more. You can go up to them and they act like they really were that person and they talk like they did in pioneer days. There is a big stone mausoleum there with a pretty young woman who tells the story of being killed by a horse on her wedding day and being buried in the mausoleum. Of course, she's not the real bride. The real bride's been dead for years!

Alice, age 11

53

WHAT DOES THAT MEAN?

Memorial Day

Say it: Mem-OR-ee-al Day

A day in late May when people honor men and women who have died in wars.

You may hear someone say, "My family always visits the cemetery on Memorial Day."

Your town will probably have flags on the graves of these women and men. You'll see special ceremonies on television.

It is also a day when many families go to cemeteries and put flowers on the graves of their loved ones who have died. Your loved one doesn't have to have been in a war to have you go to the grave on this special day.

Memorial Day is sometimes called DECORATION DAY (dec-or-A-shun day) because graves are decorated with flags and flowers and other things that are special to the family. Some families take teddy bears or angels and put them on the graves as decorations.

Story:
For my family, Decoration Day was quite an event. My mother and my aunts had gone to town and bought lots of plastic flowers. They took the flowers to three different cemeteries in three different little towns. After they put the flowers on graves – really decorated those graves – we all gathered at a little park in the last town and had a picnic.

Joy Johnson

54

Memorial Fund, Memorial

Say it: Mem-OR-ee-all Fund

A Memorial Fund is money given to the family in memory of the person who died.

You may hear someone say, "I was glad they chose his school to receive his memorial fund."

Often the funeral home will have a little sign about the memorial fund. The sign will say where the family wants the money to go. It may say something like, "The family requests memorial funds for our town's hospice program," or "Memorial funds will go to the Cancer Society."

This is a special way to honor the person who died and to show the family you care.

A MEMORIAL may be a large and famous place people come to see.

You may hear someone say, "We visited the Washington Monument."

It is built in memory of someone who died. One of the famous memorials in Washington, DC is the Vietnam Memorial that remembers and honors the soldiers who died in the Vietnam War. If you drive along the interstate highway, you may see a sign that says, Dwight W. Eisenhower Memorial Highway. Dwight Eisenhower was a United States President who arranged for the interstate highway system to be built in our country.

There are small memorials along highways, too. Small crosses with flowers and sometimes a person's name on them mark the place where someone's loved one was killed in an accident.

Memories

Say it: MEM-or-ees

Things you remember about your person who died.

You may hear someone say, "I put my grandmother's things in my memory box. I will always have good memories of my grandmother who died."

You may remember your person loved lasagna or baseball and you. You may remember some sad times, too. Memories are a way to keep that person alive in our hearts.

We remember how they looked and smelled. We remember how they laughed and how their voice sounded.

Some children make a special memory box using a shoebox. They decorate the outside of the box with pictures or art. They put things that remind them of their loved one inside the box. One boy made a box after his grandfather died. He put in Grandpa's favorite fishing lure. He put in a picture of the two of them together. He added his grandfather's watch Grandma had given him. He tucked in a copy of the funeral service program and Grandpa's fishing hat. He could open his memory box any time and think about Grandpa. Maybe you can make a box like that to help you remember your person who died.

I noticed how our tiny stitches now held together all the separate quilt squares. It was then I realized that the memories of my father were also threaded tightly within me, so nothing could ever really take him away.

A Quilt For Elizabeth by Benette Tiffault

Miscarriage

Say it: MISS-care-ege

When a baby growing inside its mommy dies before it is time to be born.

You may hear someone say, "After my mom had a miscarriage, she was sad for a long time."

A lot of the time, doctors and parents never know what made the baby die.

Miscarriages are not anyone's fault. Nothing you did or said or thought could make the baby die. Some kids say they felt bad because now and then they didn't want a new baby. Most kids feel that way one time or another. Feeling that way didn't make the baby die.

Even though you never got to hold the baby, your family had a lot of love for the baby.

This means your mom and dad and everyone in the family is probably sad.

"Grandma, why did our baby die," I asked. "Did I do it when I patted too hard? Sometimes I didn't want a new baby." Grandma gave me a big, soft hug. "No," she said. "The baby didn't die because you patted Mommy's tummy too hard. Nothing you said or did or thought could ever make Baby die. It's nobody's fault. It just happened. I don't know why."

No New Baby by Marilyn Gryte

Mourning

Say it: More-ning

How we show people we are grieving.

You may hear someone say, "She has been in mourning for almost a year now."

Imagine your grief – all your feelings about the death: sad, mad, scared, worried, confused. Imagine all those feelings in a big box. Now imagine opening the box and letting the feelings out. When the feelings of grief we hold inside come out, that is called, mourning. Mourning is what you do with your grief.

When you cry about the person who died, you are mourning. When you sit quietly in your room, you are mourning. When you get so mad about your person dying you hit your pillow, you are mourning.

Everyone mourns in different ways. Some people sit and think a lot about their loved one. Some people are restless and cannot eat. Some mourners seem upset or sound mad.

You may hear someone who is sad say, "I'm sorry. I didn't mean to scold you." Then you know that person is mourning.

Confused: It hit us real suddenly. We weren't prepared for it. We weren't ready at all. I was real sad, real confused, like why did this happen? How? My brain was really confused. I couldn't figure out what was going on.

Alex, 10
After a Suicide by The Dougy Center

Mourning Wear

Say it: More-ning Ware

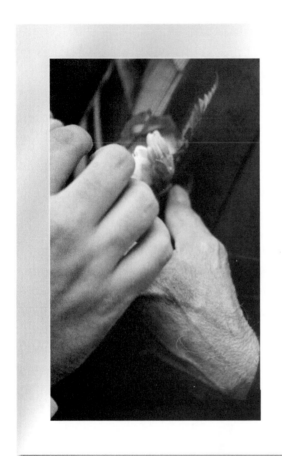

Clothes or jewelry people wear to a funeral to let others know they are mourning.

You may hear someone say, "I got this little black ribbon to wear on my suit to show I'm sad since my mother died."

It is not done much today, but in your great-grandparent's time, women whose loved one had died wore black clothing for a whole year. Men wore a black band around one arm. Today a lot of people wear black to funerals. Today, there are special pins and bracelets you can wear to tell people someone you love died.

In some other countries, people wear white to funerals. In Hawaii, people wear very bright clothes to celebrate the life of their loved one.

Some Native Americans cut their long hair very short after someone died. They wore plain and dark clothes for a year. At the end of one year, their hair was long enough to braid again. On a special day people came to their home and brought bright clothes for them. Their year of mourning was over. It was like a YEARMARK. It marked the end of a year of sadness.

Story: My great grandmother was a Fox Indian. When her husband died, she cut her hair. My mother said it looked as if she had shaved her head it was so short. She had a dark dress with dark beads on it. She wore that almost every day, washing it by hand at night. She said every morning when she looked in the mirror and saw her hair, every day when she put on that dress, she thought of her husband and knew he was dead.

Nellie Bear

Mystery

Say it: MISS-ter-ee

Something that cannot be explained or understood.

You may hear someone say, "We don't know what happened. His death is a mystery."

When a child or young person or a parent dies, people often ask, "Why?"

Sometimes there are no good reasons for a death. It is hard to understand why some things happen.

Some angry people make up reasons such as, "The doctor was no good." Others may say, "It was his time to die."

But WHY does everyone want to know about the mystery of Death? Have you ever gone into a dark room where you couldn't see anything? Maybe you were scared until you turned on the light. Maybe people ask What is Death? because they're scared of Death. Maybe people ask because they want to know why beautiful things die. Maybe people ask because the get really sad and miss the person they love.

What is Death? by Etan Boritzer

60

National Cemetery

Say it: Na-shun-all SEM-a-tare-ee

The United States government promises burial to every person who has served honorably in the Army, Navy, Air Force, Marines or Coast Guard.

You may hear someone say, "On our vacation to Washington, we went to Arlington National Cemetery and saw President John Kennedy's grave and the Eternal Flame."

There is at least one special cemetery like this in every state.

In some cemeteries a general who was very important may be buried next to a sergeant only known by his or her family.

Some graves in national cemeteries are very old. Most MARKERS are alike because the government gives the marker to the family. Husbands and wives of those buried in the national cemeteries can be buried beside the soldier when they die.

Story: There were rows and rows of white crosses. My mom and I found my dad's grave and after awhile I let the balloon we had bought go. It sailed into the air and I liked the smells and the wind and the whole feel of the cemetery. I could have stayed there a long time. It felt good.

Janna, age 10

Obituary

Say it: Oh BIT-you-air-ee

A brief announcement in the newspaper that tells about the person who died and plans for the funeral.

You may hear someone say, "This is her obituary. Do you want me to read it to you?"

Obituaries tell people when and where the funeral or memorial service will be held. Obituaries say the person who died is, survived by and lists the names of family members. Survived by means members of the family who are still living.

It may read like this:
Roy Millard is survived by his wife Mary, daughter Joy and grandson James. He was born in 1898 in Union County, Iowa, and died on November 16, 1962. Before he retired, Mr. Millard was a letter carrier for more then 40 years. His service will be at Hanson's Funeral Home at 10AM Tuesday.

Obituaries talk about when the person was born, what they did for a living and hobbies. Some obituaries have a picture of the person who died, too. We learn a lot about the person when we read the obituary.

The short statement in the newspaper telling who died and when and where the funeral will be are called DEATH NOTICES (deth no-tiss-is).

Story:
My father died when I was a young mother. I helped my mother write his obituary. It was very important to her. She would cut it out and keep it for as long as she lived, then I would keep it. Now I am nearly 70 years old, and tucked into my journal is a copy of my dad's obituary. It is old now and yellow with age and it is precious to me.

Joy Johnson

Old Age

When people have lived a long, long time and get very old, their bodies wear out and finally stop working.

You may hear someone say, "He lived a good life."

Some people do not expect family and friends to be sad when someone very old dies.

One boy said, "My great-grandmother died when she was 90 years old. No one asked how I was feeling or said they were sorry she died. She may have been old, but she was my GreatGran!"

Sometimes when a person gets very old, they are tired of living. Some want to die. Some do not. It all depends on the person. Everyone is different.

Sometimes when an older person has been sick for a long time and wanted to die, we feel relieved. We are thankful they are not in pain and hurting anymore.

And sometimes, we wish they could have lived a lot longer.

There is grief and mourning with every death. Sometimes it comes right away and other times it takes awhile. We may be relieved or glad the sickness is over then after awhile we miss that person. When an old person dies, we can be grateful for a long life and we can still be sad that person is no longer living and with us.

Story: We were teenagers when our grandma died. She was 85. She said she was "old and cold" and that's why she wanted to be cremated. We took some of the quilts she had made and draped them over chairs at the front of the funeral home so people could see them during the visitation and during the service..

Jenny and Janet

Orphan

Say it: OR-fan

A person whose mother and father are both dead.

You may hear someone say, "The most famous orphan today is Harry Potter." Harry had to go live with his aunt and uncle in a cupboard under the stairs.

Usually, when we use the word "orphan" we mean a child, but anyone of any age is an orphan when both parents are dead.

Years ago, if someone in the family could not take care of the children whose parents died, they were sent to an ORPHANAGE (OR-fan-age). This was a group home with other kids whose parents had died or could not take care of them.

One of the interesting parts of our history is about The Orphan Train. From 1853 until early 1900's trains filled with orphans from the eastern part of the United States rumbled across the country through the farmlands of the Midwest and Heartland. Children on those trains were taken to a place in each town where the train stopped. Farm families and city families met the children and adopted them. Many went to live on farms and help with the farm work. Some went to very loving, caring homes. Others were simply used as workers in factories or farms. There may be a book in your library about the orphan trains.

Today, most children whose parents die are cared for by other family members. Very few go into foster homes or group homes. It's important to know that even when bad things happen to you, there will always be someone to love you and take care of you.

Story: This young boy in tiny West Branch, Iowa, lost his mother and father before he was 10 years old. For awhile he lived on a Native American reservation in Oklahoma. Then he moved to Oregon to live with an aunt and uncle he did not know. Years later, this orphan helped save many children from dying from starvation after World War I. He always remembered what it was like to be hungry and alone and to miss his parents. Herbert Hoover was President of the United States from 1929 to 1933.

Pall

Say it: Paul

A special cloth that is put over the casket in church.

You may hear someone say, "The priest placed a pall over my grandmother's casket." Or "The tragedy cast a pall over the whole city."

Sometimes the pall has a cross on it. Sometimes the pall is white. Sometimes it is black. Not all churches use palls. When they are used, a pall covers the casket so you can't see it, whether it's fancy or plain. A long time ago, a pall was a cloak or cape soldiers wore. When a soldier died, another soldier covered him with his pall.

Today, family members or friends who carry the casket after the service are called pallbearers.

Pall is also a word used to describe the sadness people feel after a special death.

Story: As the train, nine train cars long, carried President Lincoln's body along train tracks lined with thousands of mourners, one newspaper said, "A great pall settled over the crowd standing with heads bent, tears streaming." The president's casket, covered with a black pall and bearing the presidential seal, could be seen through the windows of the train.

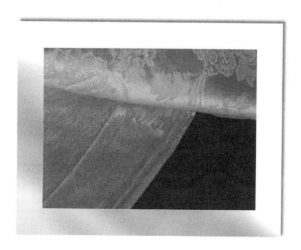

Pallbearers

Say it: PAUL-bear-ers

People chosen by the family of the dead person to carry the casket.

You may hear someone say, "She was a very popular woman with a big family. Her eight nieces were her pallbearers."

Sometimes pallbearers carry the casket to the front of the church when the funeral starts. They carry it from the funeral to the funeral coach. The funeral coach will take the body to the cemetery. At the cemetery, the pallbearers will carry the casket from the funeral coach to the grave or into the mausoleum.

Being a pallbearer is a great honor in many families. In some places, pallbearers carry the casket on their shoulders. In other places, pallbearers carry the casket at their sides, holding onto the handles. Usually there are at least six pallbearers, but a family can choose as many as it wants. The casket is very heavy, and the body inside makes it even heavier.

When some people the family would like to be pallbearer are unable to carry the casket, the family names them HONORARY PALLBEARERS (HON-or-air-ee PAUL-bear-ers). This says they are recognized as special friends of the family.

Today pallbearers are often called CASKET BEARERS (KAS-ket Bear-ers) since the cloth called a PALL that covers the casket is not used as much.

Story: My grandpa had really loved his church. I always thought it was too big and too scary. His funeral was big with a lot of people, but the church was so big, it looked like not many people were there, even though there was. The nicest thing was this soft white cloth that covered the casket. Grandma went up with me before the pallbearers brought the casket down to the front of the church. We put a single red rose on top of the cloth. I liked that.

Lucy, age 12

Pet Death

Say it: Pet Deth

When an animal or fish we love and who has lived with us dies.

You may hear someone say, "It was just a dog." But that's not true. Your dog or your cat or your bird or hamster or any pet, was part of your family. You may also hear people say, "I miss my cat so much. She was my family."

The death of a pet is an important death. A lot of times, children first learn about death when a loved dog or cat or fish dies. More and more, people consider our pets as part of our family.

If your pet dies, you can have a small funeral. Maybe you can plan some things to say or some songs to sing. Maybe you can have a special box with memories of your pet in it, like the collar and tags. You can keep pictures of your pet, too.

The very first book about death ever written for children was ***The Dead Bird*** by Margaret Wise Brown. In it, children found a dead bird. They buried the bird and said special words. For a few days they brought flowers and put them on the little grave.

When animals we love die, we're very, very sad. They loved us and we loved them and that love never dies.

Our big dog, Rafferty was so sick he could never get well. He couldn't even walk. We all three lifted him onto the vet's table. We put our hands on him and touched him. It was kind of like we were giving him a last hug. I got right by his big beef-breath face. "Goodbye, Raff," my mom said. "So long, buddy," my dad said. I couldn't say anything. I just looked at him. The vet gave him a shot, and Rafferty closed his eyes. "That's it," the vet said. My best friend was dead.

Remember Rafferty by Joy Johnson

67

Questions

Say it: KWEST-chuns

We ask questions because we want to know something. **Questions are ways to find answers to things about which we wonder or worry.**

You may hear someone say, "The funeral director answered all the children's questions."

Some of the questions you may want to ask are:
>Why did our person die?
>What happened?
>Can I go to the funeral?
>What will the funeral be like?
>Does every one in the whole world die at some time?

It's very important that you find someone who can answer all your questions honestly. There is no such thing as a silly question. The only silly question is the one you DON'T ask.

>*One afternoon Grigor's mother was waiting for him after school.*
>*"Where's Grandfather Hurant?" asked Grigor. "What's wrong?"*
>*"Grigor," said mother in a quiet voice. "Grandfather Hurant is in the hospital."*
>*"Why? What happened?" Grigor asked. His heart beat fast.*
>*Then he asked, "Can I see him?"*
>*"Yes," mother said. "He's been asking for you."*

Grandfather Hurant Lives Forever by Susanna Pitzer

Reincarnation

Say it: Ree-in-car-NA-shun

The belief in some religions that when the body dies, the spirit returns later in another body.

You may hear someone say, "I feel as if I knew him in another life."

This is a very old belief and comes from religions which began in countries far to the east of us.

They believe that the soul, or part of a person that lived, goes to a special place to learn what it needs to know about its next life.

They believe that after awhile, that soul is born again as a tiny baby and will work to always be better and good. That soul will work on finishing learning how to love people, help the world, and finish becoming a full, wonderful being.

People of the Hindu and Buddhist religions believe in reincarnation. They believe that after Death, a person's soul is born into a new body and a new life and that any thing which the Soul (or person) did not finish in her or his old Life can be finished in the new one. Hindus also believe that after the Soul has gone from one Life to another many, many times, the Soul will one day be finished with all the things that it has to do and will join the Biggest Soul anywhere – God.

What is Death? by Etan Boritzer

Ritual

Say it: Rit-chew-all

Something we do over and over again is a ritual.

You may hear someone say, "Taking flowers to her grave is a monthly ritual for us."

Brushing your teeth before you go to bed every night is a ritual. Getting dressed every morning is a ritual, too.

Families have their own rituals. Maybe you have turkey at Thanksgiving every year. Maybe you dress up and go trick-or-treating on Halloween. Maybe you open holiday presents at a special time each year. All these things are rituals.

A funeral service is a ritual. The way the service is done can be a ritual, too. Bringing food to the family is a ritual. Maybe your family visits the cemetery every MEMORIAL DAY.

A ritual done only once is still a ritual. It gives meaning to a special event.

If your pet died and you buried him and said special words over the grave, that is a one-time ritual. It means something to you. It makes you feel better. It's comforting and comfortable.

Story: Every year at Christmas time, my grandmother and I went shopping. We bought clothes in my Grandfather's size. He died about five years ago. After we bought the clothes, I helped Grandma wrap them in nice paper. We'd drive to a shelter for homeless people in our town and give them to the man who was in charge of it. He would give them to men who really needed clothes. After we left the shelter, Grandma and I would go for some ice cream together. It was our special ritual and I loved it. I'm going to do it, even when I'm all grown up.

Lisa, age 10

Sorrow

Say it: SOR-roe

The feeling of sadness you have after a loss or death.

You may hear someone say, "That was such a sorrowful song!" That means the song is very, very sad and you feel sad when you hear it.

Sorrow is kind of like sadness that lasts a long time. If you lose a toy you really like, you get sad. When you find it a little while later, the sad goes away. After someone dies, you can be sad a long, long time. That is sorrow.

There are many changes. I wish things could be the way they were. Sometimes I get really angry. I just have to let my feelings out. I feel better after that. Crying helps, too. Sometimes I feel so sad, I don't know what else to do. Once in awhile the tears just slip out and I don't really know why. It is embarrassing when that happens. I try not to do it, but when I do it is okay.

Sam's Dad Died by Margaret M. Holmes

Suicide

Say it: SUE-a-side

When a person kills himself or herself on purpose.

You may hear someone say, "My uncle died by suicide. I wish he had asked for help and let us know how really sad and worried he was."

There are a lot of reasons people do this. Some people feel so sad, angry or confused they do not want to live any more.

Killing yourself is never a good thing. It makes your family and friends feel very sad. You can find help for your problems and your sadness. You can find people who will care for you.

People who suicide don't realize how sad their family will be. Sometimes they think their family will be glad they are dead. That is never, never what happens. A family is always, always sad and wish they could have helped the person.

Families feel terrible after someone dies from suicide. Some people try to pretend it was an accident. It's always better to be honest when someone ends their own life.

Sometimes people don't really mean to kill themselves. They go too far in trying to complete suicide and can't stop it. One dad said, "My daughter took too many pills. Then she decided she didn't really want to die. She came into our room and woke us up. We took her to the hospital, but a few days later she died anyway."

Other times, it's clear that person wanted to die.

Sometimes more than one person in a family kills himself – even though years and years can pass between suicides. If someone in your family dies by suicide, that doesn't mean you will. You know already there is help when you need it and killing yourself isn't the answer.

Some people's bodies get sick and don't work right. And sometimes a person's mind doesn't work right. They can't see things clearly and they feel the only way to solve their problems is to take their lives – to kill themselves. However, this is never a solution to problems; the only reason they thought of it is that they weren't thinking very clearly.

How Do We Tell The Children? By Dan Schaefer and Christine Lyons

72

Terminal or Terminal Illness

Say it: TER-min-all

You may hear someone say, "My uncle is terminal. He's going to die." Or, "My grandmother has a terminal illness. She will die soon."

When some people get sick or have a disease, they do not get well. A disease is something that works on the whole body. It can be a virus or bacteria (like a germ only even tinier.) Most diseases can be helped with medicine or other treatments.

When a disease or illness gets really, really bad, people get so sick the organs in their bodies stop working and they die. When we know someone is going to die, we say they are terminal or terminally ill.

Terminal is another way of saying, "the end." Airplanes "terminate" at an airport. That means they end their flight there. The airport itself is called a "terminal" or "the end of the journey."

Being terminally ill, or terminal, is something like that. It means the person is coming to the end of their journey here on earth.

Some people go into a deep, deep sleep before they die. This is sometimes called a COMA (Ko-ma).

And there may come a time when I won't be able to talk to you, Megan, but I'll ask your mother to let you come then, too. Because when I smell the lilacs and hear the doves I'll know you were here and in my heart I'll say, "A kiss for my little Megan, to send her on her way."

Lilacs for Grandma by Margene Whitler Hucek

Trauma

Say it: TRAH-ma

A really big, scary hurt is called a trauma.

You may hear someone say, "This is terrible! This is a real trauma."

If you break a leg, doctors say you have a leg trauma. When death happens suddenly or by murder or suicide, families have trauma. It's scary. It's unexpected. When children are abused or hurt badly by people they are TRAUMATIZED. When a child's family member is murdered, the hurt and shock and fear are TRAUMATIZING. When there is a trauma in the family, there is a lot of stress and worry and fear. But just like grief, families can get through trauma and come out stronger.

When something terrible happens, it may not seem real at first. This is called "shock." Feelings seem frozen and people may act as if nothing has happened…or find it hard to believe something has happened. Or…people may have strong feelings and do strange things. They may feel and act crazy for awhile.

When Something Terrible Happens by Marge Heegard

Urn

Say it: Ern

A metal, wood, glass or stone box or jar that holds the human cremains after a body has been cremated.

You may hear someone say, "My grandmother's urn has a beautiful picture on it."

At first, the cremains may be placed in a cardboard box until the family picks out an urn.

Actually, any pretty jar that has a lid can be an urn. Most of the time, though, families pick out an urn at the funeral home. There are many kinds and they all look nice. Usually there is a place where the name of the person who died can be along with their date of birth and date of death.

Sometimes families keep urns in their homes on a shelf or table. Sometimes families bury the urn at a cemetery. Sometimes families keep the urn in a mausoleum.

In many ways, the urn is just a tiny casket. It holds what remains of the body of the person who died. The cremains in the urn are called cremains or CREMATED HUMAN REMAINS.

The ashes are finally put into a beautiful jar. The jar is called an urn.
If your person's body is cremated, your family will have a special place for the urn.
Maybe you can see the urn and ask more questions.

Tell Me, Papa by Joy and Marv Johnson

Vault

Say it: Valt

A big box made of cement or concrete or steel that holds the casket after it is buried.

The casket fits right inside the vault and rests there inside the grave.

You may hear someone say, "No water can get to that casket through that vault."

The vault protects the casket and the body inside. The vault protects the casket from water and dirt. It keeps the casket safe and dry. It also helps the ground above the casket look nice. If it weren't for the vault, the ground would sink in around the casket.

Sometimes the space where a body is kept in the MAUSOLEUM is called a vault. Some families have their own mausoleums and these may be called family vaults.

The old-fashioned word, "vault" means a secure place in a business or bank. Bank vaults are where the money is kept safe from robbers. Cemetery vaults are where bodies are kept safe from the weather and dirt.

At the cemetery, the casket holding the body is lowered into the ground. Waiting for it is a large cement box. This box is called a vault. It protects the casket and keeps it dry. The vault is shut and sealed.

A Child's Book About Burial and Cremation by Earl Grollman and Joy Johnson

Visitation, Viewing, Wake

Say it: Vis-a-TAY-shun and Vew-ing and Way-kek

Special times when people visit the family and, maybe see or "view" the body. Usually this is held the day and evening before the funeral.

In some places this time is called a WAKE or CALLING HOURS. It is usually held in the funeral home. People sign a guest book and talk to the family of the person who died. There will be hugging and handshakes. There will be some crying and some laughing, too. People tell the family how sorry they are their loved one died. They share memories of the person who died.

A long time ago, people called this time a "wake" because before we had embalming and hospitals and doctors, friends and family would sit with the body to see if the person would wake up. It also meant someone stayed "awake" all the time, day and night, with the body.

Some people think viewing the body is very important. It lets us see, deep down inside us, that our person is really dead.

There is nothing to be afraid of at a viewing. The body will look as if it's asleep; but we know sleep is very different from being dead. The body will be in the casket and it will look very nice. You will probably see some make-up on the face, even if the body is a man's. The hands will be folded and the body will fit nicely in the casket. You can chose to look at the body if you want to. There's nothing scary about viewing a body. It's a way of respecting and honoring our person. It's a way of saying goodbye and thank you.
You can even say, "goodbye and thank you" out loud if that feels right to you.

Story: My father didn't look like my father at the viewing. He had been sick for so long and had lost weight and looked very pale. He was in a lot of pain before he died, so at least he looked peaceful and relaxed. People walked up to the front of the funeral home where the casket was open. They looked at my dad then turned around and came to be with my mother and me. I hadn't wanted to go. I had dreaded it. But we saw people we hadn't seen in a long time. We laughed and hugged and people told stories about Dad that I had never heard before. It was really a very nice time.

Joy Johnson

77

Widow or Widower

Say it: Wid-oh and Wid-oh-er

A lady whose husband has died is a widow. A man whose wife has died is a widower.

You may hear someone say, "My grandmother has been a widow for years. There are a lot of widows and widowers in her group."

The word, "Widow" comes from an old, old word, "Verdere" (Ver-DARE-a). Verdere means, "to separate." When a husband dies, his death separates him from his wife. When a wife dies, her death separates her from her husband.

Story: I always thought of widows and widowers as being old people. But when my dad died, my mother was only 32 years old. She joined a group called, "YWWs" – it stood for "Young Widows and Widowers" and everyone there was under 40 years old. I learned you can be a widow at about any age.

Jenny whose dad died when she was 10

78

Will

A legal paper that tells everyone what the person who died wanted done with money and important things after their death.

You may hear someone say, "He left my mother several things in his will."

A person's will can say how much money they want each family member to have. A person's will can say what they want done with precious things they own.

One person usually sees that the dead person's wishes are carried out. That person is called an EXECUTOR (x-CEK-you-tor).

The more things and money a person has, the more complicated the will can be. Some people have LIFE INSURANCE – (life-in-shur-ants) special money that comes into the ESTATE (es-tate) after the person dies. The estate means everything the person owned.

If a person dies without a will, they are said to be INTESTATE (In-TES-state). This can mean it will take a lot longer to take care of that person's money and things.

Some people set up TRUSTS (ter-usts) or TRUST FUNDS. The will puts money in a special fund and that money can only be used for what the dead person has said it could be used for. Some people leave trusts for children and grandchildren to use to go to college. Some people may get a certain amount of money each month from their trust fund. Some people are given all the money in the fund when they get to be a certain age. The people who take care of the fund are called TRUSTEES (ter-ust-ees).

PROBATE (pro-bait) is a special court of law that makes certain all the bills of the person who died are paid. Probate courts work with the executor to see that the dead person's wishes are carried out. They make sure children of the dead person are cared for properly.

A person who gets something from the estate – who is listed in the will, is called an HEIR (air). That is why some important things like artwork and jewelry are call HEIRLOOMS (air-looms).

You may hear several things when it comes to wills:
> "According to the will, my dad got Grandpa's coin collection."
> "My mom is really busy. She's the executor of Grandmother's estate."
> "We won't know how much money we will have until after the will goes through probate."
> "The life insurance paid all the burial costs."

We went to the lawyer's office and he read my grandmother's will to us. She had four children and each one of them got the same amount of money. She even left some to us grandkids to use in college. She put that money in a trust fund, which meant we could only use it for college – nothing else.

Jeremy, age 14

About the Authors

Shown here are Paris Sieff, Joy Johnson, Janet Sieff and Harold Ivan Smith

Harold Ivan Smith

Harold Ivan Smith is a wordsmith, storyteller, and grief educator at Saint Luke's Hospital in Kansas City, Missouri, and for the American Academy of Bereavement. He is a graduate of The Mid-America College of Funeral Service, George Peabody College of Vanderbilt University, and has a doctorate from Asbury Theological Seminary.

Harold Ivan is a Fellow in Thanatology, recognized by the Association for Death Education and Counseling. He has pioneered in the use of children's books with adult grievers. He leads Grief Gatherings--innovative storytelling groups at Saint Luke's Hospital in Kansas City.

Among his many books are *When a Child You Love Is Grieving, A Long Shadowed Grief: Suicide and Its Aftermath, Grief-Keeping: Learning How Long Grief Lasts*, and *A Decembered Grief.*

Joy Johnson

In 1978, Joy and Dr. Marvin Johnson founded Centering Corporation. Since then, Centering has become a well-respected, worldwide grief resource center. She is the author of *Keys to Helping Children Death With Death and Grief,* published by Barrons in New York and *The Very Beautiful Dragon* series published by Centering Corporation.

The Johnson live in Omaha, Nebraska, and have six children and seven grandchildren.

Paris and Janet Sieff

Paris Sieff is almost 12 years old. She illustrated her first children's book, *Where's Jess?* when she was only seven. She enjoys taking acting classes, singing, bass lessons and hopes to have a future in theater.

Janet Sieff is the mother of the talented Paris Sieff. She loves to design children's books for Centering Corporation and articles for *Grief Digest* magazine.

To order the books quoted in this resource go to www.centering.org.